M000201948

Before Long

Auralee Arkinsly

HUM007000 **HUMOR** / Form / Parodies

HUM026000 **HUMOR** / Topic / Travel

EV010 Gift Book: **ANNIVERSARY EVENT**

BUS002000 **BUSINESS & ECONOMICS** / Advertising & Promotion

BUS036060 Business: Investments & Securities: **REAL ESTATE**

HUM004000 **HUMOR** / Form / Jokes & Riddles

HUM001000 **HUMOR** / Form / Comic Strips & Cartoons

Before Long 2019
Auralee Arkinsly
Publisher: Capture Books
All Rights Reserved.
Lb.capturebooks@aol.com
5856 S. Lowell Blvd. Ste 32-202
Littleton, Colorado 80123
Font: AidaSerifa-Condensed
No part of this book may be reproduced without
the express consent of the publisher, Capture Books
ISBN 13: 978-1-7327536-2-4 hard cover
ISBN 13: 978-1-7327536-3-1 ebook
ISBN 13: 978-1-7327536-4-8 paperback

To the real
Ernst and Esmé
who exemplify
sincere devotion and good humor in
a confounding contentment;
not to mention
their display of creative
hospitality to invite me into the ride.

ૐ

And, to my award-winning realtor-mom who raised her
children by negotiating the discontent of
homebuyers and sellers.

Ernst and Esme decided it was time to find a place to belong. "What kind of place?" Ernst asked.

"I've always liked a big old-fashioned house." Esme mused.

Before long, they found one.

The gable-house perched on a hill in a grand old style.

It came with trees in the backyard that would bear fruit.

The two were very excited.

Almost immediately, Ernst mentioned, "Have you noticed how sparse the internet is here?"

"Oh, no, dear!" Esme hemmed.

"More time for picnics?"

They invited all of their friends to
a house painting party and celebrated the big move
with a housewarming.

They bought baby chicks and built a pen for them.

Soon they would have hens laying eggs.

Before long, Ernst and Esme's fruit trees were laden with reds, yellows, dark greens, and oranges

"What in the world are we going to do with all of this produce?" Esme said.

"Let's make pies! Lots, and lots of pies!

For everyone!" Ernst suggested.

"We can sell them at the crossroads."

"By, the way, have you noticed the web of worms?"

"Eww! Dear, I hate worms." Esme groaned. "Really?"

Fruit began to fall. The orbs rose in fragrant piles. The piles began to ferment. Fermenting fumes rose to their nostrils.

When Esme's ire also rose, her voice peaked.

"Why does a nice orchard have to come with all those swarming little fruit flies?"

"I'm too tired to work and then clean up this fallen fruit every day, honey." Esme pursed her lips.

Ernst piped in, not to be outdone. "The rooster's crowing at four a.m. is kinda driving me crazy."

He exaggerated just a little bit to get the point across.

Maybe this house, with all of this land, is too big for the two of us," said Esme, sighing.

Ernst agreed.

"Let's move!"

Before long, Esme found a home in the city. There was a shimmering rooftop pool.

The commute to work would be five minutes!

A man was lounging beside the pool with his girlfriend in her bikini. Ernst and Esme looked past the sparkling water and over the railings to the sidewalk far, far below. Their flesh tingled.

Making plans with friends in the bustling nightlife, and walking to sports arenas and trips to the mall, all this kept their days happy and bright. Except "bright" became slightly overwhelming when, on game nights, the stadium lights poured through their windows.

Of course, taking an elevator up to their apartment seemed slightly industrial, and moving guests to-and-fro via an elevator was less than ideal even though the walls were padded.

"I wish we had just one extra room for visitors," said Esme looking around. "That's the only thing."

Actually, they found *another* thing. It was when they swung their legs over their bikes and headed towards the bike path.

Horns honked, "Move-it! Move-it!"

They forgot to look before turning left.

Screeching tires startled them. Horns, smelly exhaust, and revving traffic stalked them.

"It's not as fun as I thought it would be," said Ernst.

"Dear, let's go to a movie instead," suggested Esme.

They locked up their bikes and went into a cool theater.

But, when they exited, Ernst's padlock had been hacked, and his bicycle was missing.

"You go ahead," said Ernst. "I'll catch up on foot." Esme refused.

She didn't want to separate from Ernst in the big city. It was a long way to walk home in the disappointment.

"I'm not sure I like city life," Ernst said upon arrival at their doorstep. "One of us is going to get hurt." He rubbed his feet. "Do you have blisters too?"

Esme laid her head on Ernst's shoulder. "Let's move."

Before long, the couple found a town that seemed ideal.

The bungalow's classic trim was darling.

No elevators.

Not too many steps.

They set up their library and looked forward to cozy evenings reading together.

At first there was sheer quiet, no noise, but in the wee hours of morning, a train hooted and hollered from the railroad tracks which were only a mile away.

Both awoke.

"Dear!" Esme moaned. Ernst and Esme's heads plopped back on their pillows and they stared at the scalloped ceiling in their bedroom, wondering.

But they stuck it out.

Esme learned that her favorite food, a variety of pie, was being served in a restaurant on main street.

Before long, she began the habit of walking to the coffee shop where she could help market, and sample, her neighbor's home baked pies from an internet café table.

"Wish I'd had a pie baking partner a couple of years back," she said.

Ernst also found a job in their new town.

Every day after work, they walked together to main street to order from one menu or another.

"Do you think the water here tastes slightly like mud?" mentioned Ernst. "Maybe the county needs a new water purification plant."

"Dear! Tax hikes!" Esme slapped the table and spilled her drink.

"I sort of miss home-cooked food," Ernst told Esme. "All of this going out to eat has made me gain fifteen pounds, and just look at you!" Ernst squeezed Esme's hips.

"What?!" Esme pulled her husband's hands from her body.

She sucked in her gut. "You were the one who wanted to move here."

"Have you made any friends?"

"Not really."

"Me either. Is it my waistline?"

Ernst pulled Esme to the picture window to look outside. "See our mistake, hon? It's election season. Notice our neighbors have signs in their yards that oppose ours?"

Ernst ran his fingers through his hair. "We should've checked the gerrymandering map before election season."

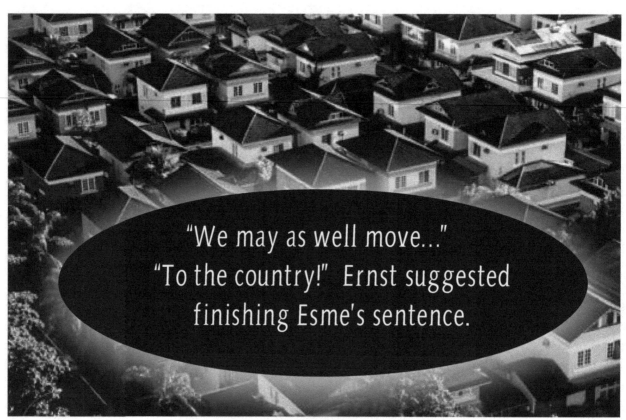

"We may as well move..."
"To the country!" Ernst suggested finishing Esme's sentence.

Before long, Ernst and Esme followed their new realtor to a fine brick house situated on a wide prairie. A cattle fence surrounded their acres of land. The neighbors were mere dots on the horizon.

"It needs a lot of work!" Ernst kicked at the debris.

"Well, I'll get my girly figure back." Esme sauntered up to her husband. "Not a restaurant around."

"Not even a pizza delivery?" Ernst peered out the window.

It wasn't but a month before they realized that their budget for gasoline and car repairs had risen with the dust clouds between their exit gate and the grocery store.

They bought a
puppy for
company.

Walt's funny mug
under his one
loppy ear

made Ernst and
Esme wonder
whether they
were really
feeding more
of a ravenous
cartoon.

One day though, Walt was chasing a fox, he stumbled into a gopher hole, and Walt broke his leg.

Of course, the upset gophers raised an alarm. They dove for their tunnels.

Since Ernst was the only one at home, he had to run for the truck, back it up, lift the eighty-pound pet - howling and whimpering - into the seat.

Ernst drove to the nearest vet.

"Oh, guess what? The vet sees to minor people injuries, too." Ernst mentioned this when he called Esme.

"Horse pills for humans? What if we got seriously hurt?"

Ernst sighed. "Perhaps we need to find our tribe," he suggested.

Esme considered.

When Ernst and Walt returned, the couple listed some growing concerns.

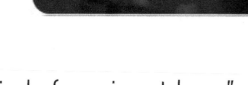

"The radio only plays one kind of music out here."

"And, it isn't ours," they said.

"I wasn't cut out to be a rancher, anyway," Esme huffed.

"Only Walt enjoys the smells of the meat packing plant."

"Okay, let's go find our tribe, get outa' the country, and find some fresh air!"

Before long, Ernst showed Esme a spacious log cabin on the hillside with four pine trees. Their best friends from school lived in the subdivision.

Also, there was a theater and elementary school. On Monday evenings, a local symphony practiced in the community center.

The meandering tarmac road made for lovely bike rides and evening walks together with Walt.

In autumn, aspens turned tangerine and lemon hues, delighting the couple.

They held hands as lovers do and grinned. Now, they could start a family.

Up came winter. Up came the shivering wind, whistling through the pines. And...

They discovered there would be no one joining them.

Funny thing, winter came to stay. The snow piled so high that Esme couldn't shovel a path to the mailbox.

Ice on the rolling tarmac prevented cycling, and most important, careful negotiations to and from work had to be observed.

From November through January, it wasn't stadium lights pouring through their windows, but holiday lights - from both sides. (You see, the neighbors had entered the community contest for best Christmas display.)

Gawkers surrounded Ernst and Esme's home. Their street became a traffic grid. They could only escape on foot.

As soon as the land warmed up, Esme decided to host a book club, al fresco.

Though...right after she set the table in the yard, a pollen storm decided to host a little party al fresco as well.

La-Lah!

Yes, she and Ernst had found their tribe, yet said tribe went on the warpath. "You should cut down that stand of trees." They said. This pollen is blanketing the neighborhood!"

Haven't these trees been here for years?" Esme frowned.

"Yes, but if you were really our friends, you would take action," said the tribal spokeswoman.

Costs were not a tribal expense.

"The pollen only bursts for two weeks out of the year." Ernst reminded the tribe.

"And, besides, aren't trees good for shade and for oxygen, birds and squirrels, and mulch, and craft projects...?"

By then, their tribe had begun to wander away.

"And, snakes!" members of the tribe called over their shoulders.

"And vultures!"

"And fires!"

"Snakes?"

"Vultures?"

"Fires?"

One day, the sewer backed up in their lovely home.

Esme called a plumber. The work involved digging up the sewer line. Ernst called their insurance company for help. Their insurance did not cover pipe breaks.

To cover the costs, they needed to take on a second mortgage.

At one decimal too many, Ernst and Esme couldn't afford this shiny new budget. They would have to sell.

$20,000.00

Before long, Ernst and Esme found new jobs... far-far away. There, they made a list and handed it to a realtor.

✓ Homey design.

✓ No wormy fruit trees.

✓ No pollen trees.

✓ No funky smells permeating the air.

✓ A cleared, clean sewer and clean water.

✓ Full radio and internet service.

✓ Friendly and Responsible Community with Independent voters.

✓ No loud, regular, constant noises.

✓ Safety from snakes, fires, vultures and villains.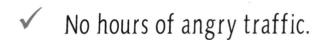

✓ Nearby gas stations and grocers. $$

✓ Walkable streets and trails.

✓ No hours of angry traffic.

Just to be sure they added...

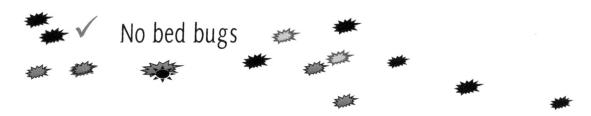 ✓ No bed bugs

Their cunning realtor found a home
with a view over water.

"Everything on your list checks off here." She said.

"Wow. Everything?"

"In fact, I called the police for any disturbances at this
address, and I can assure you that this has never been a
drug house. No burglaries, no noise issues, and never a
murder."

"Wha...?! A murder? You can check that?"

"You can, and I did." The cunning realtor reassured them. She sat them down and opened the contract to produce an offer.

Although there was an abundance of pollenating trees, they didn't mind now that the tribe was left behind.

They couldn't wait to dig their toes into the sand.

Sunsets and sunrises provided a romance they hadn't experienced in a while.

Esme began taking pictures of the reflections of clouds, of the rising mists, of the boats, and...

Walt played with children.

Walt was a kid magnet.

A neighbor invited them to go out on their boat, so off they went.

Fun hours one weekend turned into parties every weekend. The couples spent meals together and late nights on the breezy porch overlooking the water.

"I can't seem to get anything done," Ernst exclaimed. He got up from the floor and began looking frantically, pushing around the papers covering his desk.

"Oh, dear," Esme agreed snapping closed their bank register. "We *are* going broke!"

"I was going to finish my list of courses at the college, but where's my list?" Ernst rubbed his shoulder.

They looked at each other with a familiar dreamy expression. "Maybe we should move."

"Where to? Haven't we tried every ideal situation?"

"We haven't tried Spain yet."

"Are you kidding, Esme? A whole new culture?"

Esme threw up her hands. "Dear! There isn't a perfect house to be found in the whole universe!"

Ernst sat down. He folded his arms. "Moving is expensive."

Esme sat down too. She picked up a pen and began to doodle. "Have we learned anything?"

Ernst chewed his lower lip.

"We've learned how to sell produce and pies.

But, we don't like worms and flies," he said.

"We've learned how to sell produce and pies from a café on our laptops," offered Esme.

"We've learned that we like to ride bikes and take long walks together," he said. "But we aren't city dwellers."

"True.
We've learned that we like clean air and a quiet life..." offered Esme.

"But not too quiet," said Ernst pointing at Walt.

Esme nodded at Walt.

"We enjoyed renovating a house."

"Yes, Ma'am. And, we've learned that a tribe goes with the territory. Tribes can morph... somewhat," said Ernst.

"I think we should gather some courage and just tell our lovely neighbors that we have some education to consider, that boating once or twice a month is plenty for us."

"Of course."

"We should be kind about it, because we love them."

"But, maybe, we could stay here-not move-if we just stick with a plan."

"Yes. Good fences make good neighbors."

Ernst put his hands on his hips. "I'll make that registration for class tonight. It will be lots of work to reach our goals..."

Esme finished Ernst's sentence, "because we've been distracted..."

"but now we are finally settled.

We have a real home," said her husband.

"Though the closets are very small..." Esme made a face, her eyes widened. "It's home, but it's no pie in the sky."

"Maybe we can turn the empty bedroom into a big storage closet." Ernst suggested.

"There'll be no white Christmases..."

"Perhaps we can travel to our families and friends for the holidays." Ernst put his arm around his wife. "Think we can figure it out?"

Esme took a long walk. She saw many things in nature that weren't exactly perfect, but they seem to belong where they were planted.

Maybe it's time to plant our feet.

She watched intricate seeds and pollens wafting on the breeze.

She watched the waves lap at the shoreline.

She hurried home.

Before long,
Ernst and Esme
decided to...

buy a 5,000rpm road bike and waft in the wind.

"With protective leathers," said Esme.

She placed the order.